PETRUSHKA

A CURTAIN-RAISER BOOK

Petrushka

Pictures by
JAN KUDLÁČEK

FRANKLIN WATTS, INC.

575 Lexington Avenue • New York, N.Y. 10022

Text by Olga Hejná
English version based on translation by Vera Gissing
Graphic design by Jan Solpera
Designed and produced by Artia

Library of Congress Catalog Card Number: 78-106162

Printed in Czechoslovakia by Polygrafia, Prague
SBN 531-01927-6

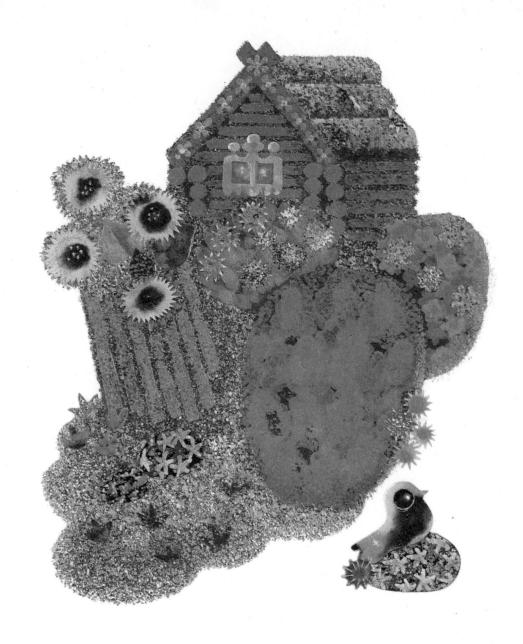

THE STORY AND THE BALLET

    PETRUSHKA is a great ballet — the result of a true collaboration between the composer Stravinsky, the artist Benois, and the choreographer Fokine, all working under the master-mind of Serge Diaghilev. Stravinsky and Benois are credited with the libretto, which is based on traditional puppet plays.

    It was first produced for the Diaghilev Ballets Russes in Paris at the Théâtre du Châtelet on June 13, 1911, with the fabulous Nijinsky as the tragic Puppet-who-perhaps-was-not-a-puppet, Karsavina as the flirtatious and silly little Ballerina whom he loved, Orlov as the flashy Moor who won her away, and the great teacher Cecchetti in the mime role of The Showman who pulls the strings to make his puppets dance, and does not believe that perhaps they can live a little.

The first and last scenes of the ballet are set in the great square of St. Petersburg in 1830, at a fair in winter. Originally Fokine used over 100 people of all ages, types and characters, in these scenes, and for the first time in ballet he used only movements natural to those characters to create his gaily seething crowd. The more true to life they could be, the more fantastic by contrast would the puppets seem to be who were the heart of the story. Fokine is rightly known as the father of the modern ballet.

PETRUSHKA has been danced all over the world: the Diaghilev company itself gave it in Paris, Monte Carlo, Vienna, London, New York, Buenos Aires and Barcelona. Fokine re-staged it for the Original Ballet Russe, N. Y., in November 1940, and for Ballet (now American Ballet) Theatre N. Y., October 8, 1942, with Irina Baronova (Ballerina) Lazowski (Petrushka) Richard Reed (Moor) and Sion Semenoff (The Showman).

This is a very ambitious ballet. It is expensive to stage, for it takes a large cast of accomplished dancers who can also act. Nicholas Beriosoff staged it for London's Festival Ballet in 1950 with Anton Dolin in the title role. Serge Grigoriev revived it for the Royal Ballet at the Royal Opera House, London, in March 1957 with Alexander Grant as Petrushka, Margot Fonteyn as the Ballerina and Peter Clegg as the Moor.

Felicity Gray

The children of St. Petersburg
      Adore the puppet show!

They cheer the Moorish Warrior as
      He fiercely strikes the foe.
They clap the Ballerina doll
      As round and round she whirls,
Showing off her frilly skirt
      And tossing back her curls.
But when the Skeleton appears
      Whose scythe is Time and Death,
His grinning skull looks frightening —
      The children catch their breath.

At last the one they love, the clown,
Skips gaily in — and tumbles down!
Oh, how the children laugh and shout
To see Petrushka knocked about!

He is the hero of our book.
      This tale from long ago
Tells how Petrushka, blown by winds
      Of fortune to and fro,
Fulfilled his destiny at last
When 'mid the snowflakes whirling fast
He came to old St. Petersburg
      And joined the puppet show.

Once upon a time a small boy called Mishka sat in a wooden house playing happily with a rag puppet.

"Petrushka. That is what I shall call you — Petrushka!" said the boy, hugging him.

At first the puppet could not understand. "He is talking to someone called Petrushka," he thought. Then suddenly he thought again, "Could it be *me*? It *must* be me, for no one else is here."

Then the boy hugged the puppet even
tighter, and skipped round the room, singing:

"Here is the stove which bakes our bread
And here's Petrushka Floppy-head.
Here we go round my Granny's bed
And here you go flying, Floppy-head!"

The puppet felt himself thrown through
the air to land on the big soft eiderdown.

So Mishka and the puppet romped about
till Grandmother appeared at the door. "Do
you know," she said, "I pricked my finger when
I was making your puppet! That means he'll
have more than his share of bad luck, poor
dear." She looked at Petrushka so fondly that
he could not help winking back. "But he has
a merry mouth," she said with a smile, "so
I expect he will somehow wriggle out of any
corner."

Mishka went hopping around the table
on one leg, shouting: "He will wriggle out of
anything, Grandma!" Just then the boy tripped
over a pail and splashed some of the water
out of it. Petrushka flew from his arms right
into the wet. But when Mishka slipped and
knocked the pail over, Petrushka was washed
along on a big wave to the very edge of the
puddle and close to the stove.

"There, you see, Grandma, he wriggled
out of *that*, didn't he?" said Mishka, laughing.
"He got wet but finished up right by the

stove!" He helped his Grandmother wipe the floor, while Petrushka sat drying.

There was always plenty of hustle and bustle in the wooden house, always the smell of cooking and baking, and the merry music of a harmonica to dance to. The evenings were the best time of all, when bearded men and plump women came to sit round the table and tell stories. Petrushka listened spellbound till his tired eyes closed in sleep.

Up in the loft lived five kittens, four shes and a tom. Petrushka and the boy had

found them abandoned in the street one cold winter's day. They had taken them up to their warm loft and looked after them well, bringing fresh milk every day and playing endless games with them.

But one sad day, it was the early autumn, when school begins, Mishka was sent to school in St. Petersburg, and it seemed as if he forgot all about his rag puppet . . . Time passed, the kittens grew up and the four of them moved next door. Only the grumpy tabby tomcat called Alexander stayed.

Petrushka was always by Grandmother's side, joking and tickling her to try to make her smile, but Grandmother had grown frail — as light as a feather — and she kept sadly gazing into the distance, as if she were preparing to fly away.

It was at about this time that a strange man came to the house. He had bushy eyebrows, sharp, greedy teeth, and breath that smelled of beer. When he came into the house he brought in with him the chill touch of a sad and stormy world which had never before invaded the snug little home. Comfort fled before him.

The moment he entered he began to shout that the house was his, that he had bought it and everything in it. He didn't want the tomcat Alexander around, so he shoo'd him away roughly. He said even Petrushka was his and grabbed the poor puppet by his legs,

letting him hang head downwards till finally he dropped him on the floor.

That night Petrushka said to himself, "Enough is enough! I am not staying here any longer. I shall run away. Grandmother has vanished, just as if the horrible stranger had blown her away, but she is probably hiding with a friend nearby. Alexander has disappeared and I shall go, too."

The puppet tried to cheer himself up by thinking of the rhyme the boy had sung, but it was hard not to cry; would he ever see dear Mishka again? Perhaps he could make his way to St. Petersburg and find him.

That very same night Petrushka slipped

through the front door of the wooden house into the street to meet Alexander. The tomcat, wrapped in his fur coat from head to toe,

was waiting for him just round the corner;
and so began the tiring long journey, in the
bitter cold, which they hoped would end in
St. Petersburg.

They wandered for days and nights, but
they just could not find St. Petersburg. Perhaps it was because black clouds covered the
moon, or because freshly fallen snow hid all
the paths; perhaps it was because a thick
mist rose from the ground, shrouding the whole
world. Whatever the cause, they lost their
way.

After a long, exhausting journey, Petrushka
and Alexander came upon a small deserted hut.

"Never mind," said Petrushka, "we'll stop here and have a good rest and a sound sleep; then tomorrow we shall find St. Petersburg with no trouble at all. It can't have just disappeared from the map!"

Alexander did his best to look miserable, lifting his wet paws and shaking the mist and dampness from his furry coat, to draw Petrushka's attention to his plight. Then he purposely began to cough and sneeze very loudly, as if he had caught a very bad chill, and was in no fit state to travel farther.

And when the puppet took no notice of all this fuss, Alexander grew cross and said: "I am not taking another step, not for anybody! Who knows anyway what sort of welcome I would get in St. Petersburg? This place is empty and suits me fine, so here I intend to stay. I am a mouser and I can settle here in style." He lifted his bushy tail proudly. "I can live here if I want to!" he went on obstinately, because Petrushka had not answered. And the puppet took him in his arms, to comfort him and keep him warm.

They came to a decision: Alexander would stay in the wooden hut and Petrushka would continue his search for St. Petersburg.

The next morning they shook hands, wished each other the best of luck, and with a parting wave Petrushka set off into the dazzling white world. "St. Petersburg, St. Petersburg, how can I find the way . . . ?"

Suddenly he heard the ringing of sleigh bells, and soon a horsedrawn sleigh came into sight. The mare was trotting gaily through the snow, with whirls of frost crystals flying from her hooves . . . "Why, I know that man holding the reins," thought Petrushka happily. "He used to visit us sometimes in our wooden house. He loved Grandmother's cakes and he had a loud laugh that made the whole house shake!"

"Mister, mister!" shouted the puppet, but the man heard nothing through his thick fur cap.

"Mister," called out the mare, slowing down, for she had caught sight of the puppet and wanted to help him. "Can't you hear, mister? Someone's calling for help! A little tiny fellow, he's calling you!" — The mare turned to Petrushka:

"I am sorry, but my master cannot hear because of his cap. Do you want to ride with us?"

"Yes, yes, I want a ride," replied the puppet, nodding his head eagerly. "That is, if you are going to St. Petersburg. Or at least near St. Petersburg," he added quietly, when the mare failed to answer. Then he sighed, shrugged his shoulders, and climbed onto the sleigh. After all, they were bound to arrive somewhere! And who knows, perhaps he would be lucky, thought Petrushka, as he hid himself in a sack of poppy seed, which lay at the

back of the sleigh, sheltered from the sharp
wind.

"What is wrong? Why have you stopped?" grumbled the man to his mare. "Come on!"

"We're off again now," answered the mare, and soon they were far away across the white plain.

Petrushka fell asleep. He was dreaming of all the things rag puppets dream about when suddenly the world seemed to spin around. He heard voices, the banging of doors . . .

"Well I never, what have we here?" said a new voice. It was the deep voice of a younger man who spoke gaily, while an exploring hand fished a sleepy Petrushka from inside the sack. "Katya, come here quickly! I think I have a new playmate for you!"

So this was how Petrushka came to live with the Carpenter and his little daughter. The old man with the fur cap left him there

with the sack of poppy seed, in exchange for a brand-new chest made of oak. He never saw the puppet, for he didn't open the sack, just set it down on the bench and drove away.

Many years went by. Katya grew up, but she and Petrushka were still the best of friends.

One day Petrushka peeped out from behind a heap of curly wood-shavings and saw the Carpenter with a plane in his hand, pacing about impatiently through sawdust and a cloud of resin scent, waiting for his daughter.

"Katya," he called, "have you painted that splendid sign I designed? I can hardly wait to see it hanging outside our shop door!"

Katya winked as she passed the puppet, and handed the beautifully painted sign to her father. He took his homemade stool outside, stepped onto it and ceremoniously suspended the sign over the entrance to his carpenter's shop.

NEW TABLES AND CHAIRS —
ANY REPAIRS.
COME TO THIS SIGN,
THE BEST WORK IS MINE.
TAKE A SEAT,
IN COMFORT EAT,
IN COMFORT STAY
OUT OF THE WAY.

First the Carpenter, then Katya and lastly Petrushka proudly read out the words on the sign. The puppet liked best of all the line which said "stay out of the way," for he was forever hearing that someone somewhere was in someone's way. If a tramp sheltered for the night in a cellar, he was in the way of a policeman. If a poor woman came to the farm to do some weaving, the four children who came with her were in the way. The gipsies who stopped on the village green, the foreigner from some far country, the feeble old lady, they all needed to keep out of the way.

"If I ever go into the big wide world,

23 I will tell everybody about this," thought Petrushka. There and then he felt the urge to move on, and decided that he had already stayed too long with the Carpenter, that he had his fill of lazing blissfully amongst the clouds of wood-shavings, and that he was bored with wasting time and just looking at life. Besides, Katya had grown up, and now, instead of playing with him, she went for long walks and dreamed of boys.

So it came to pass that when the poor peasant woman again came to the shop one day with her four children, the puppet, when the smallest one was close to him, asked: "Would you like me to live with you?"

The little boy's face lit up with pleasure. "Oh yes! . . . but they will never let you go," he added regretfully, lifting up the puppet to have a better look at him. Then, oh, horror! he dropped Petrushka smack into some glue which the Carpenter had been using to stick a bow together for the woman's herbs . . . "Here is my chance," thought Petrushka. As quick as lightning he jumped onto the woman's shawl, and, as his little bottom was covered in glue, he was well and truly stuck! When the woman came to wrap up the bread and cheese in her shawl she wrapped up the puppet too without realizing it. She slung her bundle over her shoulder and plodded off.

Petrushka made himself useful whenever possible. The woman, Anya, worked in other people's houses, doing their weekly wash. If at times a reluctant housewife refused to let her in because of all those children, the voice of the well-hidden Petrushka would come floating uncannily to her ears: "What is this? Disgusting behaviour! Let them in at once or your house will be turned into an old woodshed!" The scared housewife, thinking that some all-seeing spirit had spoken, would open the door wide and welcome them sweetly, fussing round the children and giving them nice things to eat.

Petrushka, out of sight inside the bundle, couldn't help chuckling.

One day they went to the Flea Market, where old articles were bought and sold. What a treat that was! Petrushka, finding himself among an assortment of old, strange and mysterious objects, was agog with excitement. In the Flea Market you could sell almost anything; what you had and did not want, what you found at home in the attic, or what you tripped over on the road. There were moth-eaten hats, old faded mats, screws and hooks, a number of books, crooked pins and rusty tins, all sizes of nails and worn-out pails. There were some nice things, some awful things, some lost things, some found things, some puzzling things which no one recognized. You could sell an odd left shoe, or an odd

right glove, a twisted key, a hand of a clock,
a cracked old plate, a broken pan, even a hair-
less wig. It was a typical flea market and
it gave Petrushka a brilliant idea. After that,
wherever they went, the puppet would look
down from the bundle on Anya's back and
point out anything he saw that could be sold
in the market.

"A painted metal button by your left
heel! A strong piece of wire to the right!
An earthenware mug, slightly cracked, with
a red handle behind that birch tree! I believe you'll find it doesn't even leak!"

When they had found enough things to
sell, they returned to the Flea Market, spread
them out on the shawl, and Petrushka would
shout with all his might:

"*Buy a mug, it's as good as new,*
A button, polished and pretty too;
Wires and planks and string to tie,
Come and look, come and look, come and buy."

People laughed and crowded round to see the witty little fellow, and soon the shawl was empty.

One day when they were once again arranging their poor goods on the shawl, and Petrushka sat amongst rags and laces, a big figure suddenly loomed over him, clouding his horizon, and a quarrelsome voice shouted roughly: "Do my eyes deceive me? Blood and thunder, this puppet belongs to *me*!"

Petrushka recognized the voice of the man who had driven Grandmother away and taken possession of her house. A big coarse hand closed tightly around the puppet's leg and lifted him high in the air, scattering the goods clumsily all over the place.

"Where did you find him? Tell me! He is one of my puppets!"

Poor Anya, speechless with fright, looked on helplessly. Petrushka wriggled free once and would have tried to lose himself in the crowd, but the hateful hand reached out and closed around him once more.

The man stormed at him: "You can struggle and whine as much as you like, it will do you no good. You're mine and I shan't let you get away this time."

Now the smallest boy and Petrushka were both crying loudly.

"What is all this noise about?" A police-

man hurried up, scowled at the big bully of a man, then inspected Petrushka most suspiciously. With an air of importance he swayed on the heels of his enormous boots. "Let's have the truth now! Does this puppet belong to you or does he not?"

"He most certainly belongs to me," growled the man, but Petrushka kept shaking his head pitifully, as if pleading in protest.

"Why is he shaking his head then? He keeps on shaking his head . . ." stammered the policeman.

The man answered slyly: "Why, he is only made of rags! He does not know anything. He cannot think or feel. But let me introduce myself, Inspector. I am the Puppet Master."

"A Puppet Master...? And a rag puppet... it stands to reason they belong together..."

So Petrushka was left in the choking clasp of the Puppet Master, while Anya with her children disappeared as if the earth had swallowed them up.

"You are going to act in a theatre," said the Master to the puppet. "People will

be hysterical with laughter when they see your
silly nose, and that worried look in your
eyes."

The man forgot to add that he would
make sure Petrushka had plenty to look worried
about.

Then the puppet was thrown into the
wooden box which became his prison and his
room, his cage and his shelter. He was in the
power of the Puppet Master and had to do all
that he said.

"Over I go!
Nothing but tumbles —
Oh, my poor nose!
I am the clown who gets slapped.
That's the way the world goes!"

Yes, Petrushka became the clown in the
puppet show. At every performance he was
knocked about unmercifully for everyone to
laugh at. Afterwards the Puppet Master threw
him back in his box and set off once more.
They were always moving from place to place.

At last came a day when the man turned
to St. Petersburg. They were coming to the
city Petrushka had so longed to see! He had
forgotten now why he had wished to go there.
And even if he had remembered the little
boy in the wooden house who had gone away
to school, there was no chance of seeing him
after all this time. The boy was a man now.

But Petrushka felt excited. Slumped in his box, with his cheeky cap pushed sideways, he said happily to himself: "Today the world is a lovely place, because we shall be in St. Petersburg. Perhaps we are there already. And we are going to act a play, for it is Carnival time!"

Suddenly the box hit the ground with a jolt, and before the puppet realized they had actually arrived, he heard pushing and banging and a hoarse voice shouting:

"Play us some music, you fiddlers!
Strike up! In a minute
I'll open the box, hey presto!
And show you who's in it."

Petrushka heard the loud sneezing and sniffing of the Puppet Master in the frosty air, and the voices of children crowding around, jumping up at the little theatre and shouting.

Then the dark ceiling over the puppet's head was flung up and Petrushka, still confused by all the noise and commotion, jumped high into the dazzling light, turned head over heels and landed right on the stage. The children shrieked with delight.

He saw the great buildings, the lights, the noisy crowds in the snow. Then the play began.

There were many visits after that first one and it was always just as exciting.

To Petrushka St. Petersburg meant the play, and the play meant the Warrior Moor, the other puppets — and above all Holubichka. No longer huddled in the box, waiting, the puppet performers were able now to act out their lives properly upon the stage — and Petrushka had fallen in love with Holubichka. The dainty ballerina would tiptoe in, bringing a cloud of lavender scent to waft around the doting puppet. "I ache all over," she would complain, stretching and arching her back, and shaking her beautiful head. She twirled around Petrushka impishly, so that her silky hair brushed him as she passed. He had time only to blink with delight, before she proudly danced away on her points as if she had not even noticed Petrushka.

It was always the same. He would be left looking after her in dazed admiration, while she cared about him not at all.

Then he would turn and find himself face to face with the Skeleton. This old puppet, called the Grinning Terror, was always there to remind him of less pleasant things and stare at him with his wide jaws gaping in a ghastly smile.

"Excuse me," Petrushka would say, "I was so deep in thought, I quite forgot where I was." "Was I a part of your thoughts?" the Skeleton would say with a smirk.

"Naturally you were," the puppet would   36
reply, not wanting to hurt his feelings.

The Skeleton liked to think that everyone was afraid of him, so Petrushka would
pretend to be terrified. "Look," he would say,
"I am so frightened, I can't stop shaking!
Even my fleas are hopping away in fright!"

The Skeleton so enjoyed this that all his
bones rattled with pleasure.

Petrushka watched him, thinking how
very old he must be, perhaps even older than
St. Petersburg itself. Goodness knows where
the Puppet Master had found this creature,
but for years now the Grinning Terror had
been the man's constant companion. Until the
Skeleton's joints grew stiff and strained with
age he played in the theatre. If the play was
about fighting he was always there when someone got killed. He cut them down with his
scythe. But in time he became too worn out,
and the Puppet Master pushed him behind
the props and told him to sit still and be
quiet!

Today the Skeleton was grumbling about
the Master again.

"That silly old fool! How dare he say
that I am too old to act in a play! How can
a *skeleton* grow old? Tell me that!"

"Of course you can't grow old," stammered Petrushka, full of sympathy, "I really
can't see why you can't play sometimes, just
occasionally . . ."

"But I want to act *today*," insisted the Grinning Terror in a voice so fierce and threatening that Petrushka really did begin to feel scared.

Petrushka could not help wondering why the Skeleton was suddenly so insistent on playing *today*. Why today? But anyway, the Puppet Master would not allow him on the stage . . . Suddenly the puppet noticed a little flower on the floor by his feet. A tiny, pretty thing, made out of velvet. Holubichka wore a flower, and must have lost it when she was dancing around him. Petrushka picked it up

lovingly and as he held it gently in his hands,   38
a tremor ran through him like a flutter of
a butterfly. With a feeling of exquisite sadness
he began to dance and he forgot about the
Skeleton . . .

"The children of St. Petersburg
Are going to the fair.
They're going to the puppet show
To see Petrushka there."

"Now, this is a fair," explained a young
nursemaid to a bundle of fur; only a pair of
skipping feet and a hand escaping from the
fur bundle showed that inside it was an excited
child.

"Look at the streamers, look at the round-
abouts, look at that man with the beard. They
are all a part of the carnival, and here is
a toy stall full of wonderful things. Shall I buy
you a kaleidoscope? Shut one eye and look
into it with the other one. Can you see the
beautiful pattern? Now, just a little magic
turn, and you have another pattern, isn't it
lovely? This, and everything around you, belongs to the fair."

"A bear, there's a bear!" cried the infant,
tugging at the nursemaid's elbow.

'Yes! — and watch — in a minute, he
will dance!"

"And that soldier, is he in the fair, too?" asked the child.

"Of course he is! All the soldiers, the tumblers, the musicians, the gipsies, that old man with the long beard, the peasants and townsfolk and the proud Cossacks, they are all part of the fair," she answered smiling.

"I want Petrushka!" exclaimed the ball of fur, pulling his nursemaid with all his might towards the little puppet theatre.

"Of course! You can't go to the fair and not see Petrushka, can you?" said the nurse-maid breathlessly. Flushed from the excitement and the keen frost, she made her way quickly through the thickening crowds to where the little theatre stood.

"Ladies and gentlemen, come closer, gather around," shouted the Puppet Master. "Come nearer," he roared above the music. "Come and see the dark and handsome Moor perform feats of prowess, and prove his strength!"

The red curtains of the stage parted, and on the stage stood the dark and handsome Moor, a magnificent turban on his head.

"There he is, there he is, now you see him, folks," the Puppet Master kept up his patter.

"*The Moor is a valiant warrior,*
Bold and defiant,

He has the eye of a hawk,
The strength of a giant!"

The Moor, as if brought to life by this praise, flashed his white teeth, clenched his fists and stretched out his powerful muscular arms. He really was an imposing puppet!

He picked up a large coconut, raising it slowly till he held it steady high above his head. He did this three times to prove his strength, then tossed it up and caught it. At that moment the scene was suddenly transformed into a green oasis in the parched desert, with palm trees swaying in the breeze; somewhere in the foreground flashed the gleaming eyes of a leopard. The children gasped.

"Now, another scene.
Our famous ballerina!"

Before the crowd had time to recover from their astonishment, the beautiful Holubichka tiptoed onto the stage, dressed prettily in a stiff tutu skirt.

The soldiers whistled with delight, the nursemaids giggled and the rest of the audience held their breath in anticipation. The backdrop kept changing so that one minute the scene was a desert, the next minute a jungle, the next a snowy plain with a ringing of sleigh

bells to make it even more real. Then the
Puppet Master shouted:

"*Here's a chap who's queer in the head,*
Perhaps he bumped it when he fell out of bed!"

as poor Petrushka tumbled onto the stage,
and fell flat on his face. Everyone roared with
laughter. But Petrushka uttered a piercing wail.
The Puppet Master jeered at him, then in
a tearful voice mimicked the poor puppet.

While the Puppet Master made fun of
Petrushka, whining and pulling faces, Holubichka and the Moor continued to dance
merrily around the puppet, and the audience
shrieked with laughter.

"Just look at the ballerina, she has eyes
only for the Moor!"

These lines were Petrushka's cue to start
jumping around and acting the clown, sobbing pathetically. But it seemed as if he had
forgotten his part. A curious feeling came
over him: instead of acting like a puppet,
as people expected him to, he felt suddenly
that he was something more than that.
There was that strange fluttering sensation
in his chest again. Could a rag puppet have
a heart?

Petrushka opened his eyes and seemed
to see clearly for the first time. Why was it
always *he* who got the knocks and the Moor
who danced with Holubichka? And did she

enjoy dancing with that clumsy creature, or did
she only pretend to?

"Come on, Petrushka, act the clown!"
the people cried impatiently. But Petrushka
sat as in a trance, his thoughts all over the
place.

So the scene came to an abrupt end
and the Puppet Master drew the curtains
together.

Then the man's rough hand grabbed the
puppet by the scruff of the neck, and threw
him angrily into his box, and slammed the lid
over him.

Petrushka felt himself. Nothing broken?
All in one piece? Yes, he was all right, but
oh, how he longed for Holubichka! "At least
I can *think* of you, Holubichka!" sighed Petrushka. "No one can stop me thinking of
you." Sitting in the corner of his box he lost
himself in day-dreams.

"Dear Holubichka, you are as pretty as
the blossom in spring time. If only I were
as strong as the Moor! Then I could look after
you and protect you, against the wind and
the cold . . . against all cruel things . . ." and
Petrushka dreamed of all the evils he would
keep away from his ballerina.

Oh, why can't I be as powerful as the
Puppet Master? Then I would climb, with you
in my arms, to the top of the highest tower

of the town, I would lift you up and set you high above all of St. Petersburg. You would shine there, like the moon! People would stare and say: that is not the moon, that is our beautiful, shining Holubichka!

"But I am *not* big and strong, I am not powerful, I am just nobody." Petrushka sighed, and at that moment he became aware again of that fluttering in his body, as if a butterfly were trapped inside his chest . . .

Finally Petrushka, lost in thoughts in the dust of his box, floated gently away into a beautiful dream: he had a vision of his adorable Holubichka by his side, treating him as if they had loved one another for a long time and had no secrets from each other. She caressed his face with her soft hands, kissing his unlucky nose, and said: "Of course, I dance with the Moor, but all the time my thoughts are with you! Fancy you thinking I like the Moor, what a ridiculous idea! That horrid conceited show-off, he's as fat as a barrel!" Giggling prettily she faded from his dream.

Petrushka tried to call out to her to wait — to stop a minute — but no sound came from his straining throat. "Please wait," his heart was calling, but the ballerina had gone and he woke up.

"I must see her, I must know what she is doing. She can't, she must not, be dancing again with the Moor!"

He looked up in despair at the lid above him, and through a small crack of the box he saw the gleam of the Puppet Master's evil, mocking dark eye, shadowed by its bushy brow, staring down at him . . . The unhappy puppet hid his own eyes with his hands. "This man lives for only one thing: to trap me, hold me and imprison me . . . without mercy, without compassion . . ."

But what about Holubichka? Was she still dancing with the Moor? Yes. While Petrushka sat dreaming in his box Holubichka was dancing. "Is there anyone as pretty as I?" was the only thought in her head as she whirled around the stage with the Moor. "No one has such a perfect, porcelain complexion. Everyone else has a red nose except me!" Proud of herself, Holubichka jumped higher and higher. The Moor clasped her tightly as they moved faster and faster.

"How beautiful I must look in contrast to the Moor! He is so fat and I am so dainty," thought the conceited Holubichka as she greedily listened to the applause of the audience. "How they must love me!"

Everyone watched the wild, rhythmic dance in wonder. "That ballerina is practically *flying* through the air," exclaimed a young man, and another said "The Moor's belly is bouncing up and down like a balloon!"

"How closely together they dance," a nursemaid said.

"If Petrushka saw them . . ." said a child's voice.

Holubichka heard, and paused. "He would be so unhappy that he would cry," thought the ballerina. "He has always been so kind to me . . . no one else is kind. The Puppet Master is mean, and as for his . . . his Grinning Terror, when that ugly old creature stares at me, I go cold all over. But Petrushka is not afraid of him! He is nice to him, and when I am with him I am not afraid either. Petrushka is the kindest one of all . . ."

The ballerina's day-dreaming came to an end, for the Moor grabbed her again and lifted her so high that she shrieked with delight and forgot everything except the wild, dizzy whirl of the dance.

Among the props stood Petrushka watching, as white as a sheet . . . He had raised the lid and climbed out of his box.

So great was Petrushka's longing for Holubichka, and his hatred of the Moor, that he had decided to challenge him. Whatever happened, it could not be worse than being a clown — always doomed to suffer and be mocked.

It was dusk, and although snow was gently falling, the crowd in the square was

bigger than ever. The Skeleton crawled out of
a dark corner, and came creaking and rattling
to Petrushka's side.

"Just look at those two, how closely they
hold each other! Look how they gaze into each
other's eyes!" he wheezed maliciously. "What
about it, Petrushka, shall we go out onto the
stage and join the act?"

But Petrushka heard nothing. Tortured
by jealousy and love, he was aware only of
the two pairs of hands embraced in the dance.
The tiny white pair were his, *his* . . . his heart
cried in anguish.

The despairing Petrushka threw himself
upon the stage. Before the Skeleton had time
to shake his bony chin, the puppet pounced
on the Moor. Holding him by his shirt he
shook him wildly, while the bewildered Moor
wondered what on earth had happened. He
stumbled awkwardly all over the place, gazing
around stupidly.

"Just you wait!" shrieked the puppet into
the Moor's ear. "You think you can do what
you please because you're so big! You think
I'll always crouch in a corner, stay silent
and put up with everything, looking on while
you dance with Holubichka! You're wrong!
I'll give you such a thrashing!" and Petrushka's
small fists pummeled away furiously at the
Moor.

Only then did the Moor come to. He
rolled his eyes, blinked, took a deep breath and

lashed out against the nearly exhausted little
puppet.

54

The onlookers held their breath . . . the terrified ballerina rushed between the rivals, imploring them to stop.

"Please Petrushka . . . what is wrong?
Moor, please give him a chance!
Why all this fighting, Petrushka?
It was only a dance . . ."

The Moor stopped for a moment, and glared at the ballerina, who collapsed word-lessly at his feet, then, flashing his eyes, he raised his strong arms and bore down upon Petrushka.

"Help!" shrieked the girls in the crowd.

"Run away, Petrushka!" shouted a child.

But just then the Moor, grunting like a crazed animal, grabbed the puppet and hurled him off the stage.

"Oh, gracious!" exclaimed a nursemaid, "Poor Petrushka, he threw him out like a rotten apple!"

The men laughed. "Poor Petrushka, a rotten apple!" And one of them threw him back onto the stage.

The Grinning Terror, agog with excite-ment, hobbled onto the stage, his bare skull shining in the frosty night, his mouth agape

in a sickening smile. His old bones clicked as
he clapped his hands in glee.

The Puppet Master watched with satis-
faction — the unexpected performance was
a great success. He took a sip from a bottle of
vodka, gulping it loudly, then turned back to
look at the excited faces of the audience.

The terrified ballerina slowly awoke from
her faint ... What was this deafening roar
around her? It was like the rushing of the
over-flowing river Neva, flooding through
the streets after the ice had broken ... It

was the sound of stamping feet and laughter . . . and where was the Moor going, with a sword in his hands? For Heaven's sake, why was he waving his sword?

The ballerina quickly jumped to her feet. "Moor, please stop, please wait!" she begged, attempting vainly to hold him back with her little hands, to bar his way . . .

"Oh, look! Look! What a scene! The Moor, fighting our little ballerina!" hooted the crowd. But the Moor shook himself free from Holubichka and brandished his sword above his head. Consumed with rage, he darted at the puppet who defied him.

"Run — RUN, Petrushka!" cried a little child. "He has a sword!"

The puppet ran for his life, while the Moor followed furiously, slashing the air with his sword. The people were enjoying themselves. None of the spectators took the chase seriously, they were all laughing and shouting. No one tried to stop the Moor. They were all teasing Petrushka, mocking him, thrusting sticks in his way. When he tried to run off behind the curtains, the Puppet Master barred his way. The Skeleton stood by, silent and waiting.

How could Petrushka save himself? There was no escape. Now he was cornered, and at the Moor's mercy. He saw the blade of the sword flash, then down it slashed — and pierced the puppet's heart. The unhappy bal-

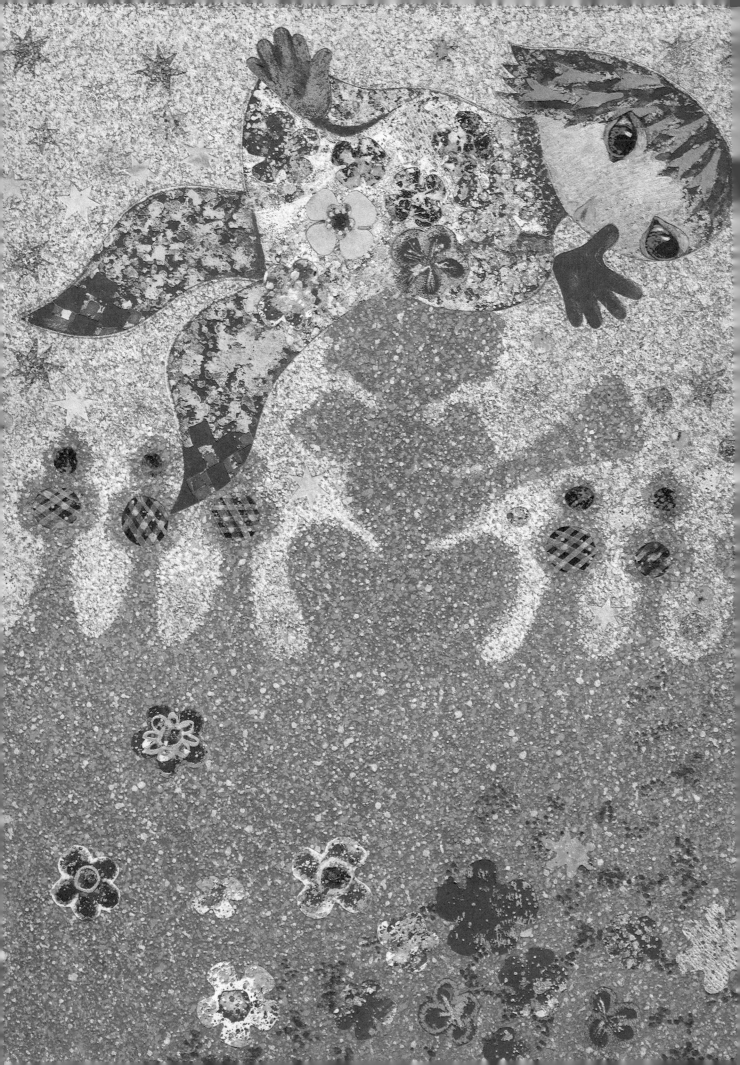

59 lerina uttered a tragic cry and fell beside him.

Poor Petrushka! As he lay there mortally wounded, scenes from the past came back to him. Suddenly he saw the faces of all the people most dear to him. He had thought about them so much and so often, and now they were all here . . . with him . . . ! Petrushka wanted to cry out: "You're Mishka, the boy from the wooden house! Oh, you were good to me, and what fun we had together! And there's Grandmother! Dear Grandmother, smiling and kind as ever . . . I do believe you are winking at me again! . . . Here comes Tomcat Alexander. (He has followed me to St. Petersburg after all.) His coat looks glossy and well brushed. He always took pride in his appearance . . .

"A little mare . . . I know you. You are the kind little mare who let me have a ride in the sack of poppy seed, and there is the man in his thick fur cap. He can hear me now. He is talking to me, saying: 'We'll give you a ride, we'll take you wherever you want to go . . .' Oh, Katya, dear Katya, and your father the Carpenter. Is he still composing rhymes? And you too, Mother Anya with your four children! How many times you have carried me in a bundle on your poor tired back! . . . But just look at you now, walking with a spring in your step, as if you were going to a dance . . ."

Petrushka's eyes misted over. It was as

if a veil of fluffy white cloud came down and
hid all these dear faces, one by one ... Yet
he was not completely alone. He saw two
outstretched arms, as white and as graceful
as the necks of swans, reaching out to him;
he felt them touch him gently and lovingly ...
but, at last, these, too, were fading away in the
gathering mist.

"He won't get up! Tell him he's *got* to
get up!"

"On your feet, Petrushka! Come and
make us laugh!"

"It's just a joke, isn't it?" a child said,
uncertainly. "He's all right, isn't he?"

The puppet lay perfectly still. The cry
went up, "He is dead, he has been killed!"

Soon the children were all sobbing: "Petrushka! Our Petrushka!" And icy wind ran
through the fair and the crowd began to break
up, shivering. They looked at each other,
puzzled, as they moved away with their weep-
ing children. Why had it gone so cold all of
a sudden? And who had upset the children
with that talk of killing? "How ridiculous!
You cannot *kill* a puppet!"

Then waves of other people who hadn't
seen the show surged forward towards the
little theatre, demanding to know what had
happened.

"You actually *saw* someone killed?"

"Who?"

"Petrushka the puppet, Petrushka the clown . . ."

"What a thing to happen!"

The Puppet Master mumbled under his breath and waved his bottle of vodka, while his constant companion, the Grinning Terror, gazed eagerly at the people, and at the puppet . . .

The little bundle of fur, sobbing bitterly, had to be picked up by his nursemaid and carried home. The nursemaid was crying, too.

"What's going on here?" demanded a policeman who had suddenly appeared on the scene.

The Puppet Master rolled his eyes, and picked up the lifeless body of the little rag puppet.

"What a lot of fuss about an old rag puppet," babbled the Puppet Master, his tongue thick with drink: "Made of rags . . . just rags . . . any old rags . . ."

The policeman frowned and scratched his head. A puppet made of rags? Well, after all, that is nothing to make a fuss about, thought he, as he turned away. "Don't cry," he said and patted the bundle of fur on the head. Soon the people drifted away to other parts of the fair to enjoy themselves; they started to munch sweets again, and sing and throw streamers. After all, this was the fair, and they had come to have a good time.

Nobody suspected that, hidden in a dark corner of the little theatre, the Grinning Terror was clapping his decrepit bony hands with joy, muttering to himself: "What deadly fun I have had today!"

"Here I am! Here I am!"

What was that? Everyone looked up. Somebody was shouting from the roof of the theatre. Who could it be?

"Look! *there* he is! He didn't die, he's alive!" someone shouted.

"Who?"

"Petrushka, of course! Hi there, Petrushka!"

The Puppet Master looked up in alarm. What were these people saying? Here was the broken puppet in his hand . . . and yet . . . there was Petrushka, alive and laughing, on the theatre roof! Was it a ghost? He shuddered and let the rag body slowly slip from his grasp. The man felt giddy. He tried to run away, but he staggered and fell. Suddenly he felt a stab of pain in his hand. The Skeleton's scythe had cut his flesh. How it pained him! How it burned! While the Puppet Master lay cursing the whole world, the Grinning Terror clattered away and was lost in the darkness.

And above the fair, Petrushka, the irrepressible, brave Petrushka, danced and sang as he always would. His spirit would never die. Petrushka would live in the hearts of the children of St. Petersburg forever and ever.